The Wyche

Curriculum

Designing a Curriculum
for the 21st Century

Geoff Rutherford

The Wyche Curriculum – Designing a Curriculum for the 21st Century
Copyright © 2012 by Geoff Rutherford

Printed in England by Little Inky Fingers
Churcham Business Park, Churcham, Gloucester

Preface

This book has been written with a dual purpose. Primarily it is hoped that some of thoughts contained within these pages will add something meaningful to the debate about the curriculum. I have been asked on many occasions about aspects of the Wyche Curriculum and have therefore taken the opportunity to put into written form some of the thinking and principles that lie behind the teaching and learning at the school.

The second reason came out of the school's link with Gofu Juu, a primary school in Tanzania. I first visited the school in 2008, I was struck by the beauty of the country, the warmth of the African welcome and a strong sense of community that I remain desirous of for our own country. However as we toured the school I was shown into a tiny room where there lay a meagre bowl of a thin white watery liquid that was set aside to feed the 170 orphans in the school. These children are left to fend for themselves and I was informed that the small cup of maize and water mix was likely to be their only meal of the day. It was one of the few times in my life when I felt totally emotionally overwhelmed, and upon returning to the UK the school established a charity called Wychumvi that seeks to feed all the children in the school daily.

This book therefore not only provides an opportunity for the school to articulate the rationale behind its curriculum in written form, but in addition all the money from the sale of each book will be sent to Gofu Juu to support the many children whose lives have been both blighted by Aids and yet are enriched by the support and giving of so many in the UK.

Contents

CHAPTER 1

A CURRICULUM FOR THE 21ST CENTURY

The Curriculum: Traditional View

There would appear, at least in educational circles, to be an understanding that the curriculum is generally well known and well set. The received wisdom is that it is a collection of specific academic subjects that have stood the test of time, many dating back to the time of ancient civilisations and that these are therefore taught in schools to children of appropriate age. More than this many hold to the belief that they can articulate the curriculum in full because it is outlined in a document entitled "The National Curriculum" which resides on their office shelves. A cursory look through its pages would lead one to believe that between 9am on Monday and 3.30pm on Friday teachers should deliver a series of lessons covering the ten prescribed subjects. Then adding a little R.E., a dose of citizenship, a few assemblies and a sprinkling of a foreign language, the school curriculum and the school week is virtually sorted.

The Curriculum: The National Curriculum's View

There are two counter arguments to this and interestingly enough both of them are found in the early pages of the National Curriculum document itself.[1]

---

[1] *HMSO (2000) The National Curriculum Document. Aims, Values and Purposes p10ff*

The first is a statement about the ever changing nature of the curriculum. Whilst most of us tend to view the subjects and their content as rigid and fixed and therefore not open to debate, the introduction's very first pages state that *"The curriculum itself cannot remain static. It must be responsive to changes in society and the economy"* The curriculum's perception of itself seems to counter the view that the content is fixed and its subject's constrained. It seems that in its inception the curriculum was designed to be organic; the notion that the curriculum is set in stone should be an anathema to those who teach as much as it was to those who wrote the original document.

The second is a statement that draws out the difference between the School Curriculum and the National Curriculum. The notion that the curriculum is designed solely to ensure a breadth of coverage across ten academic subjects found in the National Curriculum is seemingly contradicted by the document's opening sentence. It states; *"The School Curriculum comprises all learning and other experiences that each school plans for its pupils. The National Curriculum is an important element of the School Curriculum"*. Here is the nub of all curriculum development; namely that each school should cultivate two curricula in tandem throughout the school. The School Curriculum is broad and inclusive of every aspect of school life because it includes *"all learning and other experiences that each school plans for its pupils"*; for those in the Foundation Stage this may include getting changed for PE without adult help, for others it may be learning to lose gracefully at football in the lunch hour. What this statement opens up is a concept of a curriculum much broader than most have generally considered. Far from the National Curriculum being solely a document that standardises the curriculum throughout the country, its clarion call is for schools to develop a curriculum that is reflective of the needs in their community. This doesn't undermine the fact that the National Curriculum is a statutory entitlement for all children; it simply acknowledges that *"the National Curriculum is an important element of the School Curriculum"* and that the school curriculum is the framework and the context in which the National Curriculum should be set.

The Curriculum: A Challenging View

The concept of the school curriculum is the backdrop upon which any true discussion of curriculum development should be set. There needs to be an appreciation that as the National Curriculum is set for all schools then curriculum innovation can only focus on the School Curriculum. This means that schools will need to engage not just with the local situation in which they find themselves but also have a grasp of the social and economic changes that are influencing the society in which their children will live and work in the future. As the National Curriculum says *"The curriculum itself cannot remain static. It must be responsive to changes in society and the economy. Teachers, have to reappraise their teaching in response to the changing needs of their pupils and the impact of economic, social and cultural change."*

It is a sad reflection that as we stand in the midst of what Historians will probably look back on in future years, as one of the most exponential periods of global change, that the curriculum stands alone in being one of the few features to remain generally unmoved and unchanged. The technological revolution has transformed every aspect of our society and yet schools remain relatively untouched. It is a salutary warning to us all that "one of the only places operating largely as it did fifty years ago would be the local school"[2], and to allow this to remain will short change generations of children in the years to come

The Curriculum: A Changing Society View

The speed of technological change continues to increase exponentially, transforming every area of society in its path as it marches relentlessly onward. It is sobering to think that as recently as 1993 there were only fifty websites in the world.[3] Yet today typing "London" into Google produces 1,900,000,000 hits delivered in 0.21 seconds. We are in unprecedented times fuelled by an information explosion such that *"a week's copy of the*

---

[2] *Making Connections,(1994) Renate Nummela and Geoffrey Caine.*
[3] *Quote from "The Struggle for the Soul of the 21st Century" Bill Clinton, December 14, 2001*

Times newspaper contains more information than a person was likely to come across in a whole lifetime in the 18th Century".[4] Whilst the number of text messages sent each day exceeds the total population of the planet. One might surmise that due to the fact that any information is but a click away on a computer or even a phone in a pocket that this would have impacted greatly on the content driven approach to learning held so sacred since the Victorian industrial age. Yet when one compares the 1904 secondary school curriculum with that of its present day counterpart one finds the only change to be that ICT and DT have replaced the lost subject of Housewifery![5]

The technological onslaught does not just mean that we simply need to make children ICT literate, for the debate runs much deeper than that. As educators we need to look at what impact the technological revolution is having on society as a whole and how it is shaping and moulding the world with increasing rapidity. A few years ago Richard Riley, the former US secretary of state, made his infamous comment that *"the top 10 jobs that will be in demand in 2010 didn't exist in 2004."* He went on to say *"We are currently preparing students for jobs that don't yet exist...using technologies that haven't been invented...in order to solve problems we don't even know are problems yet."* The children in our Reception classes may well leave higher education in 2027; which begs the question what will the world be like then and what skills can we equip our children with today that will be applicable to tomorrow? Educators have a moral imperative to engage with the future if we are truly to prepare children for the world of tomorrow rather than the world of yesterday. As Tony Blair once said *"Children cannot be effective in tomorrow's world if they are trained in yesterday's skills".*[6]

So what are the key trends and changes? As Yogi Berra once wryly observed, *"It's tough to make predictions, especially about the future."* Whilst there is much that remains hidden there are some trends we can predict with an element of certainty simply because they are already evident albeit in fledgling form.

---

[4] *Shift Happens from the original created by Karl Fisch,Arapahoe High School, US*
[5] *Gillard D (2011) Education in England: a brief history*
[6] *Tony Blair Connecting the Learning Society: DfES(1997)*

4

The job market will change beyond all recognition in future years. Whilst those retiring at present will have been in an average of two to three organisations throughout their working life when their children retire it is estimated they will have been in 18-25 different companies. By the age of 38 today's learners will have had 10-14 jobs. There will be (and already is) a shift towards portfolio working where rather than applying for jobs people apply for projects and when the project is complete they apply for the next. Technology and it's creation of the ability to work anywhere has allowed this outsourcing to flourish. This is fine, but the skill set required to thrive in this working environment is markedly different from the industrial model of the last century. Those entering the job market will need to be creative, adaptive and have the ability to re-create themselves in a series of careers rather than just settling into a "job for life" as they might have done in the past.

This is not just the future this is the present, it is just that sociologists believe these trends will speed up rather than slow down as technology pervades deeper into our society. Industry already requires a different skill set from that which was desired in generations past. The QCA undertook a study based on the principle spelt out in the National Curriculum that *'Education only flourishes if it successfully adapts to the demands and needs of the time'*[7] They asked a range of industries what they felt were the key features that future employees needed to be successful in the world of work. They came up with the following:

- Flexibility and Adaptability
- A good mix of qualifications, practical skills and personal qualities
- Good interpersonal skills
- Ability to solve problems and create new ideas
- Take responsibility and show initiative
- Apply technology purposefully

This feedback clearly demonstrates that whilst the academic and subject specialism rightly remains at the heart of the statutory curriculum, children need more than pure academia if they are to thrive in the wider world.

---

[7] *HMSO (2000) The National Curriculum Document. Aims, Values and Purposes p10ff*

The Curriculum: Subjects or People?

The most interesting and most counter intuitive aspect of the technological revolution is that it has brought the need for inter-personal skills to the fore. Whilst the science fiction writing of a generation ago predicted a completely automated digital world where life became semi-robotic in its nature, the reality is that it is interpersonal skills which have come to be the prized skill set of the day. With technology (and the rise of the manufacturing industry in the Far East) releasing manual work from the job market, Britain has become predominantly a service sector society. Networking and the building of relationships, along with the ability to think creatively and out of the box are the key skills that are currently driving our economy and it is these aptitudes that are valued within industry at present.

There has been a fresh engagement with the concept of Emotional Intelligence. Daniel Goleman's seminal work on the subject[8] has made thinking in this area mainstream; however, by his own admission[9] he accepts that he was simply building on the thinking of Howard Gardner's multiple intelligences[10] and the more academic studies of neurologists Antonio R. Damasio[11] and Joseph LeDoux.[12]

Current research, as well as anecdotal evidence, shows a clear shift in the need for young people to acquire a secure set of social skills. The IPPR study published in 2006 focused on the study of two large groups of children born in 1958 and 1970. Their findings showed *"that in just over a decade, personal and social skills became 33 times more important in determining relative life chances."*[13]

---

[8] *Goleman, D (1995) Emotional Intelligence*
[9] *http://danielgoleman.info/2011/howard-gardner-multiple-intelligences/*
[10] *Gardner, H. (1993). Multiple intelligences: The theory in practice.*
[11] *Damasio, A (2006) Descartes Error*
[12] *LeDoux, J (1999) The Emotional Brain*
[13] *Freedoms Orphans – IPPR study (2006)*

The Curriculum: Change or the Status Quo?

Guy Claxton wrote that *"If the core purpose of education is to give young people a useful apprenticeship in real-life learning, then the kinds of learning they do in school has to match the kinds of learning that people do in the wider world"*.[14] This statement is a challenge to the curriculum as we know it or rather, the curriculum as we thought we knew it. If we are to narrow the gap between the "artificial learning environment of the classroom", as Mick Waters once described it, and the real world, then we need a fundamental root and branch review of the curriculum. It will not be enough to simply take the subjects of the National Curriculum, juggle them a little and hope they land in a more cohesive format than we have at present. We need a more radical solution that redirects and refocuses what we feel children need both through their school life and beyond.

The issue with many current curriculum initiatives is that we are simply repackaging the same subjects. This is not the solution anymore than re-arranging the furniture on the Titanic would have been a good idea as it slipped deeper into the icy, cold waters of the Atlantic. The Titanic's problem was not the things on the boat, but the boat itself. And so it is with the curriculum, the problem is not the subjects in and of themselves, they are a rich source of learning, it is just that they are not often set in the correct context of a "School Curriculum" as was originally intended. Drawing further on the analogy above, the school curriculum is the vehicle that provides the contextual framework for the teaching of subjects. So when it comes to curriculum innovation, our creative energies should focus on the holistic "School Curriculum" rather than on a potentially fragmented curriculum based around individual subjects. In short rather than starting with the subjects and building up from the bottom, the process should start at the macro level of the whole curriculum and then dovetail the micro elements into the bigger picture.

As Ken Robinson says *"Every education system in the world is being reformed at the moment and it is not enough. Reform is no use anymore because that is simply improving a broken model. What we need is not*

---

[14] *Claxton, G (2010) What is the point of School?*

evolution but a revolution in education. What we have has to be transformed into something else""[15] To this end Ken Robinson might be surprised to find his views supported by Christine Gilbert, Ofsted's chief inspector, who as chair of the 2020 vision report wrote *"It seems clear to us that the education system will not achieve the next 'step change' in raising standards simply by doing more of the same; a new approach is required".*[16]

The Curriculum: A Call for Radical Change

Now is not the time for more of the same, nor even more of the same but better, now is the time to stand back, discern objectively where society is headed and seek to create a curriculum that will equip future generations to live as successful learners, confident individuals and responsible citizens, to quote Jim Rose's overarching aims in the Primary Review.[17]

My working title for this document was "The 21st century curriculum" The first time I came to save it as a document I was presented with a box which posed the question: *Do you want to save your changes to the 21st century curriculum?* I was then given two simple options: Yes or No. I know that transforming the curriculum is not that simple nor that straight forward but for those children who each day look to us to provide the rich learning environment in which they can thrive and grow, we should neither underestimate the magnitude of the task nor shirk from the responsibility of the challenge.

---

[15] *http://www.ted.com/talks/sir_ken_robinson_bring_on_the_revolution.html*
[16] *Christine Gilbert 2020 Vision Teaching and learning in 2020 review Dec 08*
[17] *Independent Review of the Primary Curriculum: Final Report April 2009*

CHAPTER 2

DEVELOPING THE WYCHE CURRICULUM

The Context

By the summer of 2007 the school found itself in a position where it felt able to develop a curriculum that reflected more closely the ethos and philosophy of the school.

To facilitate this, the governors and teaching staff met to explore this concept together. They split into groups to brainstorm ideas around one central question: *"What is it you want the school to have given the children when they leave in Year 6?"* Some years later the QCA used a similar question *"What are you trying to achieve?"* in their curriculum development tool; *The Big Picture.*[18] Such questions remain the key feature in all good curriculum planning, drawing out the foundational issue of a school's ethos and values and allowing it to then ascertain how their own curriculum can be modified to deliver them.

The meeting generated a list of skills, attributes and competencies that the school then took away and refined into what is now known as "The Wyche Curriculum".

---

[18] *http://www.qcda.gov.uk/resources/publication.aspx?id=aaf9d7bf-7043-4bd8-9bb8-438d36908984*

It was John White who proposed the seemingly counter intuitive notion that any curriculum planning that originated with the curriculum subjects themselves was, by definition, a somewhat flawed approach. The "School Curriculum" should have as its foundation curriculum aims to which all in the school can adhere. Most of these, by definition, will not be rooted in the traditional academic subjects. Indeed within the National Curriculum itself *"60% of the specific aims mentioned are about the pupil's personal qualities, as distinct from skills or types of knowledge and understanding"*[19]

As if confirming this view, it was interesting to note that it was well into the discussion before any of the groups noted that they had failed to include any of the traditional academic subjects. What was apparent was that both teachers and governors were starting with the values, aims, and purposes of the curriculum rather than pure academia. In this they were simply replicating the stance of the current National Curriculum. Whilst many turn to the "What to teach" pages in the subject sections, the power of the curriculum is found in the "What context to teach in" articulated in the early pages for it is here that the curriculum's aims and values are spelt out. As the document itself says *"These aims provide an essential context within which schools develop their own curriculum"*.[20] The Wyche Curriculum has "aims, values and purposes" at its heart and it is around these that the curriculum subjects are moulded. In this regard it would be true to say that the subjects should be subservient to the broader aims. Therefore, the process means that the knowledge, skills and understanding cease to become ends in themselves, but instead become the vehicles through which the school delivers the aims, values and purposes of the all encompassing school curriculum.

Taking the original list from the Governors' meeting the teachers set about the task of giving it some coherence. Through much discussion, the staff worked on the process of editing and sorting the attributes collating them into five main categories. These are outlined in summary below and in further detail on the succeeding pages:

---

[19] *White, J (2004) Rethinking the School Curriculum*
[20] *HMSO (2000) National Curriculum Handbook*

Curriculum Aims for the Wyche School Curriculum
Summary Version

General Ethos

1a	Key Features: Happy Memories
1b	Key Features: Enjoyment and Fun
1c	Key Features: Love of learning
1d	Key Features: Friendship and Community

Relating to Self

2a	Key Features: Self Esteem and Confidence
2b	Key Features: Reaching Potential
2c	Key Features: Developing a sense of Spirituality
2d	Key Features: Being Healthy

Relating to Others

3a	Key Features: Friendship
3b	Key Features: Understanding Relationships
3c	Key Features: Developing Relationships
3d	Key Features: Teamwork
3e	Key Features: Global Awareness and Responsibility
3f	Key Features: Cultural Appreciation

Managing Learning

4a	Key Features: Improving your own learning and performance
4b	Key Features: Communication
4c	Key Features: Application of Number
4d	Key Features: ICT
4e	Key Features: The Arts and Sport
4f	Key Features: Thinking Skills
4g	Key Features: Creativity and Problem Solving

11

Managing Situations

5a	Key Features: Managing conflict
5b	Key Features: Managing Disappointment
5c	Key Features: Managing Time and Resources
5d	Key Features: Managing Risk and Uncertainty

Curriculum Aims:
The Wyche School Curriculum

General Ethos

Key Features: Happy Memories

Our overwhelming desire is that at the end of a seven year association with the school each child should leave with a portfolio of rich and happy memories. Whilst this may appear a little nebulous to include as a curricular aim it is in fact the bedrock of the school's philosophy and encompasses everything it seeks to achieve.

Key Features: Enjoyment and Fun

The curriculum should instil within children a sense that learning is fun. They should come to appreciate that to face and overcome challenge builds self esteem and a sense of self worth and that this concept of learning becomes an experience they should come to value and enjoy.

Key Features: Love of Learning

The curriculum should engage children so they not only see a value and use for learning but come to appreciate that the concept of lifelong learning is a key component in a rich and fulfilling life.

Key Features: Friendship and Community

Schools should be microcosms of the communities they seek to serve, to this end the school should provide rich opportunities for children to develop a depth of friendship and relationships with others that they find supportive in the short term but also later on in life; it is true that many of life's most precious adult friendships spring out of those developed as children in primary schools.

Relating to Self

Key Features: Self Esteem and Confidence

The curriculum and more importantly, the manner in which it is delivered, should enhance a child's awareness of their own abilities and strengths as a learner; thus ensuring that children see learning as an ongoing process not a one-off event.

Key Features: Reaching Potential

The curriculum should instil within children a sense of inbuilt challenge that causes them to permanently strive to achieve of their best. They should appreciate the intrinsic value of always seeking to reach one's potential in every sphere of life.

Key Features: Developing a sense of Spirituality

The school has a Christian foundation and the curriculum should reflect this. Children should be given opportunities to explore their own spirituality in the context of the Christian faith and tradition.

Key Features: Being Healthy

The curriculum should provide adequate opportunities to encourage children to develop a healthy lifestyle.

Relating to Others

Key Features: Understanding Relationships

Children should come to appreciate the impact that their personal behaviour has on others and how to resolve issues of moral conflict when they arise.

Key Features: Building Relationships

The curriculum should provide rich opportunities for children to develop a wealth of relationships in differing contexts. Therefore, by definition, these should cross gender and age barriers and should emphasise the strength of diversity whilst celebrating the uniqueness of the individual.

Key Features: Developing

The curriculum should provide opportunities for children to relate to others appropriately, developing an emotional skill set that allows them to promote mature and fulfilling relationships based on empathy and a true understanding of others.

Key Features: Teamwork

The curriculum should provide opportunities for children to work in teams. This should include understanding how teams operate and the variety of roles needed for teams to be effective. They should also experience managing and being managed by others as well as developing a competence in their ability to develop the skills and talents in others.

Key Features: Global Awareness and Responsibility

The principles of global awareness allow children to take the relational skills they have developed at a local and personal level into the wider arena of caring for those they may never meet. They should appreciate that the decisions they make about their own lifestyle can have a profound effect on the lives of others around the world.

Key Features: Cultural Appreciation

The curriculum should offer children a full and rich understanding of their own heritage and culture, whilst developing a healthy respect for the cultural traditions of others. They should acquire an appreciation of the way others do things and recognise that these differences add to the richness of the world, not detract from it.

Managing Learning

It is important to clarify that these are not simple duplication of subjects found within the National Curriculum. There is a statutory requirement upon all schools to teach the National curriculum these aspects relate more to generic areas of learning. So whilst "Communication" may lean on skills taught in literacy the focus is on the art of communicating subject matter from other curriculum areas such as science, geography or history.

Key Features: Improving your own learning and performance

The curriculum should engage children fully in the learning process. Teachers should therefore teach in a manner that allows children to make increasingly accurate assessments of their own performance and help them reflect on how to improve it.

Key Features: Communication

Communication is the bedrock of human society. Successful communication builds solid relationships and is the arena in which all academic study is presented to others. Whilst the majority of work may well be in written form the curriculum should take due care to emphasise the need to develop secure skills in Speaking and Listening.

Key Features: Application of Number

The curriculum should reflect the fact that the acquisition of mathematical calculation strategies is not an end in itself. Children should apply these within a range of contexts, presenting their findings coherently and justifying, in mathematical terms, their reasoning for the conclusions they have drawn.

Key Features: ICT

The acquisition of ICT skills will prepare children to participate fully as adults in the rapidly changing technological age. More than that ICT offers children access to new ways of learning. The internet is an ever increasing rich resource of information, whilst the presentation of ideas, concepts and children's own work has been revolutionised through ICT.

Key Features: Knowledge and Appreciation of The Arts and Sport

The arts offer children a richness of cultural heritage; it gives them a wider understanding of the experience of life and is an outlet for pure creativity. A love of sport not only contributes to a healthy lifestyle but allows children to explore the principles of teamwork as well as managing success and disappointment in a competitive arena.

Key Features: Thinking Skills

The curriculum should provide adequate opportunity for all children to explore a range of thinking skills. This allows children to focus on "knowing how" as well as "knowing what" – learning how to learn. These should include the ability to reason, analyse and evaluate and should be applied across the whole spectrum of curriculum subjects.

Key Features: Creativity and Problem Solving

The ability to generate and extend ideas is, and will increasingly be, valued in the adult world therefore the curriculum should provide rich opportunities for children to explore creatively. This should not be limited to the traditional creative subjects such as Art and Design but should permeate all curriculum areas as the children explore concepts emergently.

Managing Situations

Key Features: Managing conflict

The children should develop a wealth of strategies to resolve conflict in a manner that allows them to retain their own self respect, but similarly acknowledges that those around them have a different viewpoint to their own.

Key Features: Managing Disappointment

The children should understand the importance of managing disappointment appropriately. This is of the utmost importance for where a curriculum is couched in challenge there will be opportunities aplenty for children to encounter setbacks and discouragements, yet they should learn to see them as opportunities to overcome and accept them as an integral part of the learning process, not a symptom of academic failure.

Key Features: Managing Time

Children should be able to mange their time effectively. They should be able to work towards appropriate deadlines both as individuals and as teams, handling the pressure when time constraints impact on a given project.

Key Features: Managing Risk and Uncertainty

Children should experience a curriculum that offers great opportunity for risk taking and uncertainty. The challenge to master the unknown is the doorway to true learning. Children should embrace this confidently and fully appreciate that no learning takes place without an element of uncertainty and venturing into the realm of the unknown.

These have therefore become the overarching values through which the whole curriculum is taught within the school. Hence all planning, lesson observations, and judgments made about children's progress will be measured against these. This is not to say that we don't value progress in Mathematics, English or any of the other curriculum subjects for that matter (the school's academic standards bear ample testimony to this) it is just that the school is seeking to deliver and demonstrate progress in the broader view of a more holistic curriculum. This means that the school's success, as deemed by its stakeholders, will be determined more by how it delivers on these aims and values rather than how well it achieves in the individual subject disciplines.

This approach has an obvious impact on curriculum planning. The idea that planning can remain primarily subject focused is clearly erroneous. The school needed to rethink through how it could develop a planning structure that would translate the aims of the Wyche Curriculum into secure classroom practice.

CHAPTER 3

WHAT MAKES A GOOD VEHICLE?

The Principle of the Vehicle

One of the questions I get asked more than any other is; "How do you plan for the Wyche Curriculum?" The core feature of the planning process lies in the principle of the vehicle around which the whole of the school's curriculum planning hangs.

As we developed the curriculum it soon became evident that if you centre the teaching and learning around attributes such as "relating to self", "relating to others" and "managing situations" then any form of planning that relies primarily on the subjects of the National Curriculum will not be fit for purpose. Much is made of the "Cross-Curricular" approach but in the majority of cases a more accurate description might be the "Cross-National Curricular approach". The QCA units and other schemes of work produced by government agencies or the many educational publishers often have a heavy subject discipline focus. In some cases, like the QCA units, they rely primarily on the teaching of one subject. Others rest on the principle of seeking to meld the curriculum subjects together and of course, this form of planning has traditionally taken on the title of "topic work". This is all very laudable; since we all recognise that learning is holistic and in its truest sense should break past the rather artificial divisions created by the subject boundaries. However, it was clear to us that the curriculum we were seeking to introduce was larger than just a collection of curriculum subjects brought together, albeit in a creative way.

It was out of these thoughts that we developed the concept of "The Vehicle". The vehicle was to be the driving force for the whole curriculum. It would not only deliver the attributes within the Wyche Curriculum but would also provide a cohesive framework in which to teach the subjects of the National Curriculum. The vehicle is not a "topic" in the traditional sense because it is designed to deliver much more than just the national curriculum subjects. The vehicle should provide opportunities for children to learn about the management of themselves, relationships and situations, as defined in the Wyche Curriculum. The planning process therefore hinges on the development of a theme that draws these principles into a sharp learning focus.

For instance, the teacher might decide that in studying the Tudors the children will develop a museum inviting parents and the wider community to attend. In one sense there is nothing particularly novel in that, many schools will do something similar, however what we try to ensure is that the learning throughout the term weaves its way through the key areas of the Wyche Curriculum. For instance, it would be easy to produce two life-size costumes to display in the museum and in the past the teacher may have embarked on these as a whole class project with the children contributing to them under the teacher's guidance and tutelage. Whilst not wishing to diminish the value of such a project out of hand it will be evident to even the most casual observer that such a project would neatly sidestep most of the elements of the Wyche Curriculum. To announce that only some of the children will be wearing the costume, to then design them in groups, create it together and end by discussing which costumes the class think should go through to the museum will hit many of the social and relational aspects of learning that the previous activity bypassed completely. To this end often the planning is not markedly different in terms of the end product, but the journey to get there seeks to stop off at key staging points along the way before reaching its destination.

In truth the vehicles tend to be richer than the one illustrated above simply because the museum idea still has the potential to gravitate towards a study of a curriculum subject; with the museum acting as nothing more than a showcase of the work done throughout the term. The better vehicles are those that move away from a particular subject discipline and focus solely on the principles of the Wyche Curriculum. Thus, the Year 2 class that created particulars of real houses that they visited, measured and then displayed in the local estate agents was an example of a vehicle with no specific reference to the National Curriculum. The Year 3 class designing story sacks for local playgroups, the Year 4 class setting up travel agent websites, the Year 5 class publishing and selling magazines in local newsagents and the Year 6 class selling their own inventions to local industries, are all examples of vehicles that have not had the National Curriculum as their starting point and are probably richer for it. Of course, it is easy to see how the subject skills found within the National Curriculum can be integrated into each of these examples and these in turn enrich and extend the learning. The key to successful planning is in creating a context that delivers the attributes of the Wyche Curriculum, yet a by-product is that it will provide a real-life scenario for the national curriculum subjects themselves.

Over the years it has become apparent that there are guiding principles that create a rich learning environment for the teaching of the Wyche Curriculum. The reality is that we have learnt these through trial and error, often the richest lessons coming through the error rather than the trial. The list below reflects our thinking at the present time. It is by no means exhaustive and we add to it regularly but these are the key features of what, we believe, makes a good vehicle.

What makes a Good Vehicle?

1. A good vehicle drives the whole topic throughout the term. It pulls all the threads of learning together and is not therefore a 'bolt on' at the end of the term where the work undertaken is simply showcased.

2. The vehicle should, as far as possible, replicate for children, life and learning in the real world. It will draw on processes that adults work with everyday and narrow the gap between the artificial world of the classroom and the reality of learning that occurs in the world.

3. It should seek to draw on expertise within the community. If you are writing music: use a musician; making a TV programme: get a director. These people fulfil two important functions in the process of learning engagement. Many of them are inspirational, in the sense that they have ability and skills which go beyond those within the school community. But secondly, and more importantly, they are aspirational. Whilst it may be possible for teachers to excel and inspire children in their field of expertise, they cannot be "aspirational" because when all is said and done they remain teachers. Many children say of the visitors; "I would love be like them when I grow up". In these terms there is a difference of some magnitude between being able to inspire and aspire. Inspiration hinges on what you can do whilst aspiration is founded on who you are. In our experience the latter is the more powerful of the two.

4. The vehicle will draw on all areas of the curriculum, forming a cohesive learning experience. It will certainly merge the subject boundaries, yet at the same time the distinctiveness of the each subject and its unique set of skills will be kept sharply in focus. All too often it is the subject skills that often bring freshness to the vehicle preventing the learning become dry and boring. Persuasive writing in Year 6 may not be the highlight of every child's week but when the Year 6 class wrote to Richard Hammond trying to persuade him to come to the Wyche with the Top Gear team, the quality of the writing moved onto a different level. The context may have driven the Literacy, but the Literacy was seen by the children as the means to fulfil their desire to see a TV star attend the school.

5. The vehicle will, by definition, focus on interpersonal skills, the development of team based projects and should cause children to reflect deeply on their ability to work together.
    a. They should understand the roles within teams, the leader, the facilitator, the worker etc. and learn to play to the strengths of each other. They should also gain an increasing understanding of the power of group dynamics.
    b. They should appreciate that the strength of relationships will determine the effectiveness of any task they seek to undertake.

c. They should develop a range of strategies that facilitate effective working in teams. They should learn how to resolve conflict, manage disappointment and how to negotiate ways forward as a team.

The planning of the vehicle should be skewed to achieve these. Incidentally they may come about by chance, but a curriculum where these are viewed as key objectives not by-products requires there to be a rigour in the short and medium term planning that demonstrates how they are to be secured.

6. The vehicle is integral to the success of the topic; therefore, removing the concept should cause the whole topic to implode and become a meaningless set of unrelated curriculum activities. The children should therefore be totally engaged with the vehicle and its purpose and they should see it as being the key facet in their learning. If this is not the case the likelihood is that the vehicle has become a "bolt on".

7. The vehicle is the driver for pupil motivation. Whereas in the past the motivation may have been extrinsic e.g. "rewrite the story before you go out to play", the vehicle should provide an arena for intrinsic motivation. There should be a natural striving towards excellence based on the fact that all learning will contribute to the goal of the vehicle.

8. The 'Mantle of the Expert'[21] operates on a client model where there is an outside agency that drives the project forward. Wherever possible this is a model of working that would be good to replicate. Certainly it would appear that the most effective vehicles have been those where projects have worked towards fulfilling the needs of a client. It allows for negotiation, with an outside party who in turn create a need to constantly re-evaluate the product.

9. The vehicle must be seen through to its conclusion. For example, whilst making an African Board game is good fun, to not find an outlet for its use rips the heart out of the vehicle for the children; therefore, the end goal should be well thought through in the initial planning and then

---

[21] *http://www.mantleoftheexpert.com/*

24

carried through to completion. Children have expressed disappointment when the vehicle has driven the topic but the proposed end goal has fallen away.

10. The key to a successful vehicle can simply be the context in which it is set. An idea that appears average in one context can become outstanding in another. For instance, storysacks made for the reception class in school is not as powerful as making them for the local playgroups; similarly an internally produced school newspaper is not as effective in terms of outcome as a magazine published and distributed within the local community around the school.

11. There is a growing awareness that whilst the children in the upper reaches of Key Stage 2 can maintain enthusiasm and focus for a vehicle over the course of a complete term, the younger children often need staging posts that allow them to work in shorter time frames. So whilst the overall project might culminate in a final event at the end of the term the planning needs to include additional elements to sustain the project throughout. Therefore, the Year 2 class working with Cadbury to create a new chocolate may produce confectionary products which can be used for market research mid-term. This not only adds to the ultimate objective but also adds fresh energy for the children as they work through the project.

CHAPTER 4

WHAT DOES PLANNING LOOK LIKE?

Why planning can't start with the Curriculum Subjects

It was John White[22] who first made the rather counter intuitive statement that when planning the curriculum one should not start with the curriculum subjects, but of course he is quite right. If one accepts the premise that there is a significant difference between the "School Curriculum" and the "National Curriculum" then they will, by definition, require differing formats in terms of their planning. National Curriculum planning can legitimately start with the subjects and for years prior to the current document (published in 2000) the most common format was the topic web. The topic approach sought to draw out a central theme around which the national curriculum subjects could be taught in a coherent context. This was based on secure pedagogy. It held that all learning should be contextualised and a central theme such as the Tudors allowed the national curriculum to be taught through this one context. This cross curricular approach was felt to offer the richest form of learning, an approach HMI have commended.[23]

However, in 2000 the government introduced overall aims into its revision of the National Curriculum. As John White points out *"The aims transcend specialised perspectives. They are chiefly about the sort of person that*

---

[22] *White, J (2004) Rethinking the School Curriculum*
[23] *The Curriculum in Successful Primary Schools (2002) Ofsted*

school learning is meant to foster".[24] The Wyche Curriculum is similar in that it addresses the needs of the learner rather than the content to be learnt. To this end it therefore becomes incongruous to use the subjects as a starting point for planning as they are not the means by which these aims are delivered. The National Curriculum document made a seismic shift towards looking at the learner as a learner rather than looking at the learner as a receiver of a body of prescribed knowledge. This fundamental change in philosophy should have had a major impact on the teaching profession, but history will record that alongside the introduction of the National Curriculum came the publication of the legendary QCA units. These were content driven rather than learner led and the aims, values and purposes outlined in the broader curriculum became sidelined, as schools sought to deliver what was perceived, at the time, as the validated schemes of work.

The Vehicle

It became clear that to follow the principles of an aims-led curriculum such as the Wyche Curriculum would take a radically different form of planning. We therefore developed the concept of "The Vehicle". This concept lies at the heart of all we seek to achieve throughout the school and the bedrock of all our planning.

The vehicle is the starting point for teachers within the planning process. They will design a "project" that they feel will deliver all the aims and values held within the Wyche curriculum. At this juncture there will be no engagement with the content of the national curriculum subjects, the emphasis is on developing a structure that delivers the attributes of the learner as a person rather than what is to be learnt. The teachers therefore design, what we call, a "Walk Through" of their vehicle, which basically is a skeletal outline of the project and how the teacher believes it will address the aims in the Wyche Curriculum.

This process is usually undertaken in the latter weeks of each term so the project is ready at the commencement of the following term. There is no

---

[24] *White, J (2005) Towards an aims led curriculum*

rolling programme of vehicles and no structural element to the long term planning. This was a deliberate move on my part as I felt that where the focus is on content coverage then the rolling programme is a tool fit for purpose, but if the curriculum is founded on broader principles one has to question its validity. The key to a successful vehicle is teacher engagement, enthusiasm and excitement and it is my belief that a blank canvas provides more opportunities for these to flourish.

To illustrate the vehicle planning process the following pages are the "Walk Through" produced by Jon Westwood (Deputy Head) for his Year 6 class project on Disability. The project lasted a term and culminated in a "Dragon's Den" where children presented products they had designed to a panel of experts. The numbers and letters throughout the planning relate to the aspects of the school Curriculum and can be cross referenced using the summary sheet which can be found in the Wyche Curriculum document.

About the unit

The project has been shaped by the children. Since visiting the MENCAP carol service the children showed a keen interest in disability. They wanted to design and make something that would make a disabled person's life a little easier. This will be done through a Dragon's Den style project where children will work in small groups (pairs if necessary). The project will be shaped by two strands: Disability and Design & Technology.

The idea is that whatever disability the children show an interest in they will research / contact an organisation to find out more, listen to invited guests, make contact with someone who has that disability and find out what would make their life more comfortable/easy, before setting about the DT element. The children will need to find a company that would be willing to back their idea and help them produce a prototype from their own drawing, models or design. (eg. Stella was training Jenson to undo her zip on her jacket, but he couldn't quite grasp the zip pull which caused both of them some frustration. One group may decide to explore a new zipper attachment for a dog to undo. There would definitely be a market for it and there would also be customer to trial the product).

Throughout the project each group / pair will keep a Big Book record of what they have done. A topic folder approach to record their journey. This may include some elements of their learning logs.

Learn Object	Teaching Activities	Assessment
To understand the term disabled.	**What Is Disability?** Using displays in the classroom the children will try and establish what disabled means. They will also look back at their original statements of what they believe disabled means. After discussion the children will attempt to classify the different categories of disability. *Managing Learning 4g Problem Solving*	Children able to classify disabilities into relevant categories.

Experience Disability For A Day – Learning Logs

To experience what is must be like to have a disability.

To gain an understanding of disability from someone who is employed as a carer.

The children will be given an opportunity to experience what it must be like to be disabled for a short period of time. This will include being disabled but also what it is like for a carer. There are two opportunities to explore here. Firstly the children will be blindfolded to see how they cope with being blind. Secondly there is the option of wearing ear defenders to see what it feels like to be partially deaf. Parental permission will be obtained before children are disabled due to health and safety.

However, if resources allow it would a great opportunity to see what it would be like to be in a wheel chair if enough wheelchairs can be brought to the school.

This to be explored by JW

General Ethos 1a, 1b Relating to Others – 3a, 3b, 3c, 3d

Experiences recorded in learning logs:

Disabled person

Carer

Keen Interest – Group Formation – Learning Logs

This i: re the children will need to revisit their learning logs to remember how people responded and worked last term, but at the same time I   peful that groups or pairings will be established through a common interest. The children will begin to think about which disability they would like to explore. Ultimately these groups formed will be the groups that stand in front of the Dragons at the end of the unit. Their hopes and expectations will be monitored through the learning logs. The children will be working in pairs or in threes (largest groups).

This is the first time that I am concentrating on small groups or pairs. The Wyche Curriculum has usually centred on group work. This will be an interesting study to see how much progress individuals make in pairs as opposed to groups. The other possibility is whether to pair up SEN children to provide them with the support they need throughout the project. This idea will be explored with Bill & Tom.

Managing Learning 4a, 4b, 4d

Board Meeting 1 – Company Name & Logo

Each pair or group will need to look at designing a name and a logo for their newly formed company. This will fit closely with the RE project signs and symbols. Each group will look at the current disability market and current disability logo.

Managing Learning 4a, 4b, 4e, 4g Managing Situations 5a, 5b

To understand the importance of names and logos.

Does the company name and logo reflect market and product?

Board Meeting 2 Contact – Personal – Dragons

Each group will be asked to write a letter to the dragons as seen on TV to see if they would be interested in assisting with the project. The result from this could be both disappointing and exhilarating! Watch this space!! Access can be made via media line on Dragon's Website. Business School section of the website highlights the nine key areas for applying for a design application including *intellectual property*.

(Alan & Julie Peat may be used as dragons to review children's CD Roms)
The children will also be writing to someone they know who has the disability that they are interested in. Contacts with the children will be kept to people within the school community as they may be invited to come into school and speak to the children.

There a lot of virtual contacts available through recognised BBC web pages using high profile personalities.

Relating To Others, Managing Learning, Managing Situations

To talk to people with disability to gain an insight into their world.

To und___ and the proces involv approaching someone with a new design or invention.

Letters drafted.

Nine areas of business outlined and explained.

Board Meeting 3 Find Out More

To use time efficiently and effectively	The children will be given time to research more about their chosen disability. This will also give them an opportunity to focus more tightly on a specific aid that could be designed or made to aid the process of identifying a need that will shape their design brief. This is really a time management activity where the children will have to find out as much as possible within the allocated time. A fact sheet will e produced based on their research. Discussions with some of the children will need to be had to allude to the best methods of research to make best use of time. This will depend upon pairings.	What did they know? What do they now know? Evidence – Fact sheets produced.
To research facts about an unfamiliar subject.	Additional time will be allowed to read case files as this knowledge will prove more beneficial. This could be done though guided reading with texts researched by myself and Mrs Creber.	Case studies texts for reading.

Fort Royal
Dave Palmer is happy to arrange a visit to the special school to allow children to meet and work with children who have differing disabilities. It will also provide an opportunity for children to talk to and ask questions to those who teach AND/OR care for disabled childrn he experience will hopefully get them thinking about the things that they want to design.

Steve Davies Architectural
Engineer to talk to the kids regarding disability access in new buildings. Children will do a survey of the school highlighting where access for someone in a wheel chair may be difficult. Building regulations will be looked at closely.

Worcester Blind college
Mrs Creber has worked with a lady from the blind college who visits schools and talk to children about being visually impaired. This is something that Sarah Creber is happy to set up for the Year 6 class.

Foot & Mouth Painting

To begin to appreciate barriers and boundaries when coping with a disability.

Follow up from initial research FMPA is a website dedicated to those artists who paint with their feet or mouth. The children have seen examples from this website and were astonished. It is safe to say that all want to have a go at painting with their mouth or feet. Hygiene issues to be explored.

Despite having a disability the boundaries for disabled people tend to be other people! Children need to understand that disabled people have a normal life.

Adam Taylor is keen to come into school and teach the children ART – Water Colour painting.

General Ethos 1a, 1b, 1c Relating to Self 2a, 2b, 2c, 2d Managing Learning / Situations

Learning Log entries based on perceptions of disabled people and boundaries and difficulties they experience.

End products displayed around room.

Guest Speaker – Wheel Chair Bound

24 year old wheel chair bound rugby player to talk to Year 6. Bev has a contact at The Worcester Warriors. It would be great for the children to listen to and meet someone who is young and in a wheel chair. Most of the views and perceptions of the Year 6 see elderly people in wheel ̃s, not young people.

Relating to others 3f

Communication Channels – Braille and Sign

The children will look at communication using Braille and Sign language. The class will hopefully begin to learn some of the basics. There are numerous interactive sights on the internet where you can teach yourself sign language. Mrs Harrison has a great deal of the basics and is happy to teach the class.

General Ethos, Managing Learning 4a, 4b Managing Situations 5b, 5c, 5d

Board Meeting 4a – Dissolution and Reformation

Not sure about this – but it would be interesting for some of the companies to go under (at this stage rather than later on as a lot of work may be lost); therefore merging a sister company. This would definitely promote and encourage most aspects of The Wyche curriculum.

Board Meeting 4b – Design Brief & Idea Brainstorm

During this session the children will start to think more carefully about the design brief. They will need to think about what they could design following an original design brief already shared and established within the class. Their decisions should be shaped by what they have experienced over the past few weeks – meeting and talking to people with disability, their own experiences, research and case studies.

Hopefully the children will come up with their own questions that will shape the project.

The topic of patenting will be explored. The process follows a similar route to our own way of planning a DT project.

Relating to others, Managing Learning, Managing Situations

To create a clear design brief to adhere to throughout the project.

To define problem and pose question

Ideas created need to correlate with design brief.

Misinformed decisions will need to be challenged.

Board Meeting 5 – Existing Products – Disassembly

To investigate a range of similar existing products.

To talk to people who have used the products for evaluation purposes.

Each group regardless of product will need to complete a detailed investigation of what products are already out there. The children will be encouraged, where possible, to handle these products and to look at several areas: What they are made from? How they are made, cost? Who they are made for? Value for money? This will be the disassembly part of the project from which they can commit to an idea following the original design brief.

Information gained from this vital part of the process will be used to shape their own ideas. They will need to also consider the limitations that they may encounter when designing and making a product. It may be that the children use a company or outside agent to help them make their product e.g. Brock at The Chase can form and cut plastics. But it is essential that the children produce a prototype.

It would be good to talk to people who have used some of the researched products to get their opinion and views.

Relating to others, Managing Learning, Managing Situations

Children create a success criteria list for their own products based on the preferences of themselves and of course the disabled people who use the products.

Board Meeting 6 – Ideas On the Table

Through observations the children will begin to generate their own ideas giving consideration to practical boundaries.

Intellectual Property! One way of ensuring intellectual property is to post design to yourself and not open the envelope as proof of the design.

Based on the Design Brief and Success Criteria list the children will begin to produce detailed drawings of their design, fully sized, labelled and annotated.

Relating to others, Managing Learning, Managing Situations

Detailed drawings represent the criteria from design brief and success criteria list.

Board Meeting 7 – Focussed Practical Tasks

Engage safely in practical investigations to gather and record evidence for their chosen product.

The children will be given sufficient time to explore how they might make their specific products and plan their build. The build of their product will be closely monitored and the children will continually be encouraged to evaluate their progress. They will need to use this time to continually test how they join materials so that it fits purpose considering the aesthetic and durability qualities of the product. They will also have to think about the cost implications. Some groups may need additional help from companies that manufacture certain products. It is at this stage the children may need to think about who could actually help them. This will be the largest hurdle for the children. It is my intention that all pairs will be able to make a working prototype of their design demonstrating that the product is fit for purpose. However, there may be times when the children will need to start again with a differing idea.

Relating to others, Managing Learning, Managing Situations

Board Meeting 8 – Evaluation

To continually make systematic evaluations.

The children will be asked to evaluate both their product and group dynamics through the learning logs.

Relating to others, Managing Learning, Managing Situations

Learning Logs regarding the progress of their product.

Board Meeting 9 – Professional Help & Costing

To speed up the process the children should be able to make a simple phone call to the necessary organisation requesting help. They should have made sufficient progress with their product and be in a position where their designs can be improved or processed. Help may be in the form of testing by their chosen disabled subject. Throughout the entire project at all times the children will be encouraged to work alongside their disabled subject to ask them for advice and opinions.

General Ethos, Relating to self, Relating to others, Managing Learning, Managing Situations

Board Meeting 10 – Amendments to Design & Final Product

	The children will be once more encouraged to read both the design. With the help of the disabled person the children will tweak their product before final testing.	
To continually make systematic evaluations.		
To understand the importance of quality ; inish of their uct	The group will then discuss how happy they are with their product and complete a simple evaluation of their product prior to the testing period. Headings for the evaluation will be determined by the design brief and success criteria lists.	See individual evaluations in learning logs.
	Relating to others, Managing Learning, Managing Situations	

Trial and Testing

To get realistic evaluation and feedback regarding their end result.	The product will need to be tested. In some cases this may be for a period of time or repeated testing. This will provide valuable feedback to the group. The material received back from their subject will provide a case study to be included in their final CD Rom or presentation to the dragons.	

Board Meeting 11 – Evaluations and Modifications

To continually make systematic evaluations.

Board Meeting 12 – Marketing and Copyright / Patent Pending

To understand what is involved when applying for a patent for a particular product.

Applying for a patent on line website will provide all the guidance needed to ensure that children understand what is involved. There is a school in Texas that has done something very similar, where children aged between 11 and 12 have designed something for a disabled person. It would be interesting to see what they have created and read their blogs about the different stages. Some of our own learning logs could be shared with the school.

Relating to self, Managing situations

Board Meeting 12 – Presentation to the Dragons

Depend   n the Dragons this will either be in the form of a live presentation person to person or via Skype or through a CD ROM. The idea is that the dragons choose whether or not their design is a viable business venture! The next step will be determined by how successful the products have been. If need be further steps can be taken to put one or more of the designs into commercial production!

Key Features of the Planning

The key features to point out from this planning model are the following:

1. At this stage the key is for the planning to deliver the Wyche Curriculum rather than simply being a collection of good and creative ideas that may contain some great learning experiences, but bypass the deeper aims and values at the heart of our curriculum.

2. Related to the above is the use of Jon's *"Dissolution of the groups"* which he was considering mid-project. His thinking behind this was not simply to introduce an edge to the project but related more to the need to draw out deeper aspects of the emotional and personal curriculum. As alluded to above, some vehicles were discarded as unsuitable, whereas others were able to be re-focused using the same theme and were then able to fully deliver the school curriculum

3. Whilst the planning seeks to be as thorough as possible at this stage it is impossible to predict how a topic will mushroom and develop. So it was with this vehicle, once the work had begun in earnest many people came forward offering support and help. The wheelchairs Jon was hoping to source arrived with enough for half the class to spend the whole day in them with peers acting as carers throughout the day. The Dragon's Den was hosted at the local Science Park and included a professional inventor, the head of Qinetiq (local research based firm, formerly DRA, the Defence and Research Agency), an inventor and Adam who suffered from muscular dystrophy that confined him to a wheelchair. Other contacts included a Health and Safety Officer (a grandfather of one of the children) who showed the children the impact that the Disability legislation on building regulations had on the school, as well as a parent physiotherapist who works with disabled children. There were many more links made with other individuals and organisations. Whilst we welcome these, and have come to expect them, the initial planning should be sufficient within itself to deliver a cohesive project throughout the term.

39

4. You will have observed the complete lack of any references to the National Curriculum (bar the odd cursory comment relating to Design Technology) and this is deliberate. Our early forays into this form of planning proved a challenge for some who had always used the national curriculum as the starting point. Comments were made such as "This would be a good vehicle because it has lots of Science and the DT would fit in...", yet invariably this approach made for the weakest vehicles. The key is held in the opening sentence of the National Curriculum document: *The national curriculum is an important element of the school curriculum.* The School Curriculum is the receptacle (or the vehicle) for the national curriculum; therefore, it makes no sense to start with the national curriculum. The planning degenerated into a collection of curriculum subjects, becoming no more than a "topic" similar in style to those that teachers had used for years. For many there needed to be a conscious move away from the subject based mindset into an arena where planning is focused on creating a unit of work that delivers values and aims first, and then integrates the skills and understanding found within the national curriculum.

5. From this some may draw the conclusion that the school considers the subjects of the curriculum to have little or no value. Nothing could be further from the truth. Whilst many schools have created curriculum leaders around areas of learning, the Wyche has held staunchly to the principle of subject co-ordinators. The subjects add much to the teaching and learning of children bringing unique disciplines to the teaching. It is the content of each curriculum subject that draws the learning into real life situations preventing it becoming dry, dusty and one dimensional. I am sure there is a wonderful thinking skills lesson that could be based on the old adage "How many angels can dance on the head of a pin?", but instead why not explore the question "Do you think Henry VIII was a good king?". The children would use the same thinking skills to debate and discuss but could call on secondary sources to back up their claims as well as looking at the principle of "Fact and Opinion" found in so many historical writings. For me the

national curriculum would add a dimension to the thinking that the former lesson would sadly lack.

Integrating the National Curriculum Subjects into the Vehicle

The "walk through" is monitored by the head and the deputy and when it is believed to be secure teachers will then move on to integrating the national curriculum subjects into the vehicle.

This element has proved both the easiest and the most complex in our journey. At this stage in the planning process staff enter their traditional comfort zone of integrating the curriculum subjects into the vehicle using the same principles as with previous topic planning.

National Curriculum Coverage

Whilst the integration of subjects into the vehicle was relatively simple to achieve, the greater issue came in the macro elements of curriculum planning and the issue of broader curriculum coverage. As the national curriculum is a statutory entitlement for each child schools have an obligation to ensure that all the curriculum subjects are covered in their entirety throughout each Key Stage. In truth our curriculum set new challenges in this regard.

The National Curriculum subjects fall into two categories: those that are content driven and those that are more skills driven

Skills Driven: English, Mathematics, Art, Design Technology, Music and ICT

Content Driven: Science, History, Geography, PE and RE

The skills based subjects were easy to integrate into the vehicles. This is due to the fact that the programmes of study for these subjects do not prescribe any specific content. So, using Jon's vehicle as an example, he was able to integrate the Design Technology into the project seamlessly as all he had to ensure was that the children covered the full range of skills throughout the work. Similarly they wrote letters to disabled people in Literacy, designed their pitches to the dragons using PowerPoint in ICT, their maths focused around aspects of their design work and the Art supplemented much of the work throughout the project.

The content driven subjects proved trickier to integrate. The old topic approach often drew a range of curriculum areas under one umbrella, which was itself usually focused around one area of the National Curriculum, for example, Chembakolli (Geography), The Tudors (History), Forces (science) etc. This enabled a cross curricular approach to be adopted which ensured curriculum coverage in the long term planning as the topic itself was driven by a specific subject from the National Curriculum. The vehicle approach removes the subject as the central focus and replaces it with the Wyche Curriculum. This has the potential to leave a vacuum in terms of curriculum coverage. I would love to pretend there is a quick and easy solution to this but if there is we have not found it. However, after many years we have developed the following which we believe ensures effective coverage.

RE is taught wholly discretely and no attempt is made to integrate the subject into the vehicle, except where a teacher might choose a vehicle theme that has an RE focus. To date we have not used this option.

PE is also taught discretely like RE but there are often opportunities for PE (especially dance) to become part of the vehicle, and wherever possible the subject is taught in this context.

Science has a rolling programme that ensures that there is complete coverage of the subject throughout the Key Stage. This released teachers in their planning from "having to" integrate Science. However, what we have found is that there are ample opportunities to build Science into many of the vehicles. Thus, our approach is two-fold; a discrete programme runs as a back bone, but where topics dovetail into the vehicle they are taught in this context. I would suggest that at present about half of the Science is vehicle based and half is taught discretely.

History was a greater issue because at KS2 the subject is heavily content driven with one of the broadest Breadth of Studies in the National Curriculum. To be fair I wonder whether the there is any school in the country that currently covers all the statutory seven areas required at KS2. However, when we looked for a solution the teachers were all united in their desire to ensure that one vehicle a year had a History focus. There was a consensus that both staff and pupils enjoyed history themed projects and therefore to have this constraint would not be arduous or limiting.

Geography has proved the trickiest to solve. The content aspect remains the issue and at present we have a two-fold solution. We have taken the thematic studies and each year undertake a Geography Fieldwork week in KS2 where we study the themes of Water (River Severn), Settlement (Malvern Town Centre), Landscape (Malvern Hills) and an Environmental Study within a four year rolling programme. These have proved very successful and the concentrated focus leads to a high quality of learning. Each of these weeks includes a Geographical Enquiry and takes in the Knowledge and Understanding of Patterns and Processes. In terms of the contrasting locality whilst the curriculum is covered it is not done in one concentrated topic as it might have been previously. The school has strong links with Gofu Juu, a school in Tanzania and a lot of the work relates to this locality in Africa. So whilst the programmes of study are fully covered they tend to be delivered in a more fragmented manner as they align closer to the vehicles than the more traditional topic approach which had a single locality as its focus for a term.

Monitoring Planning

From this point on in the process I suspect our systems are much the same as other schools. There is a triangulation process in the monitoring. The subject leader looks at the plans for their particular subject to ensure continuity and progression. They also check to see that the planning delivers a purity in terms of the subject, and has not been diluted by being placed in the context of a vehicle. The deputy and head then look at all the curriculum planning to assess its quality and engage either the classteacher or the co-ordinator if they feel that it is not secure.

CHAPTER 5

DOES THE CREATIVE CURRICULUM RAISE STANDARDS?

Does the Creative Curriculum raise standards?

I have framed the question with the wording most people use when they debate the issue of curriculum innovation and standards. However, the most illuminating answers usually come from the most insightful questions and I would suggest that this is probably the wrong question. The most obvious repost might be "Raise standards in what?", yet as you will have appreciated the school believes there is a lot more to raising standards than simply seeing the scores rise in two subjects, based on a test that barely lasts an hour taken by one cohort of children in a week in May. The reality is we are all seeking to raise standards, as Ken Robinson says "Why would you lower them!?", but maybe the question should be re-phrased because what most people mean is *Does the Creative Curriculum raise standards in Mathematics and English?* My answer to that in short is... "No not necessarily". In which case, the more perceptive question might be *If the Creative Curriculum raises standards, in which areas of the school curriculum does it have the most impact?* This might lead us to a more cogent answer.

The School's Journey through the Standards Agenda

The opening sentence of chapter 2 stated that *"By the summer of 2007 the school found itself in a position where it felt able to develop a curriculum".*

The import of the statement implies that there was time when the school was not in a position to develop. This was due to the fact that it was not delivering securely enough on the standard's agenda. I share this because I feel the school's own particular journey towards the creative curriculum has a great bearing on the question we are seeking to answer.

I took on the headship at The Wyche in the spring of 2000 and embarked on a single minded mission to create a school centred around a creative curriculum. Whilst the core subjects remained a key focus, I saw the SATs and the continual practicing of test technique a huge distraction to what I believed was the core purpose of education. However, it was not long before the SAT scores started to slide and in 2002 we stood on the abyss with E grades across the board on our PANDA report (the forerunner to Raise Online). There is little doubt in my own mind that the school would have been placed in "Special Measures" if it had not found itself in the fortuitous position of being mid-cycle in the inspection process.

In my defence, I would still maintain that the teaching and learning the children received in those days especially in the two core subjects was creative and enriching. At the time I was a Leading Maths Teacher (those tasked to model lessons for the new Numeracy Strategy) and the school had a reputation locally for its creative and innovative approach to the subject. We also had two other Leading Maths Teachers and a Leading Literacy teacher on the staff. The truth is that, whether we like it or not, there is a separate skill set that needs to be applied to test situations. "Don't spend too long on one question" is excellent advice for those taking exams, but of course is the complete antithesis of the resilience towards learning teachers seek to build into their children on a daily basis.

Interestingly no-one has ever called me naïve in the approach I took in those early days of headship for the simple reason that I am quite happy to describe myself in these terms before they get the chance. Whether we like it or not, we are in an education system that values the scores derived from the tests at Key Stage 2. I found myself on the horns of a dilemma and in what I believed, at the time, was a pivotal crossroads for the school and for me personally. I was aware that the system does not allow schools to stay in a place where they are deemed not to be achieving, but at the same time I did not want to lead, what I coined as a "SATs factory" nor was I prepared to "sacrifice children on the altar of SATS".

Our journey, here at The Wyche, owes much to the wisdom of some in our profession who had trod this path before me. They had all led successful schools and believed it was possible to "play the game" without selling your soul completely to the testing regime. With a major element of scepticism we embarked on a programme of drawing out the main aspects of test technique articulating them in a document called "Jumping through hoops", whilst all the time seeking to minimize the impact on the creativity of the curriculum. I am not necessarily proud of this work but it was a pragmatic response to the constraints of the testing system.

At times I wrestled with the integrity of following such a path but was heartened by the perspective of one curriculum advisor in particular. He pointed out that at the end of the day we are government employees, paid by them to deliver their agenda. Therefore, all schools have a moral obligation to "Render to Caesar what is Caesar's" and I felt this to be a good moral compass to follow in charting a way through, what can be a philosophical minefield of integrity.

To complete the story the SAT scores in 2006 put the school in the top 100 schools in the country in terms of Value Added, the scores the following year were even higher and placed the school 20th in the country.[25]

In my own mind the greatest sense of achievement has not been the results in and of themselves, but to achieve them without diminishing the creativity of the curriculum nor placing undue pressure on the children. In the early days I did wonder what the impact would be on them as the school chased the elusive Holy Grail of levels in tests. A few years ago a visitor came to the school and spotting some Year 6 children they enquired

---

[25] *I will readily accept that the school draws children from a catchment area that might make "Playing the Game" a little easier than for those schools in more challenging areas. I don't debate this aspect here but felt it only right, in the name of transparency, that I acknowledge that such an assertion might be true and that the local factors may have had a huge impact on the school's success in devising a solution.*

of them what level they felt they might achieve in the upcoming SAT test. The silence and the quizzical looks between the two children that followed showed me that whilst the SAT scores remained a focus for the school it had not become a focus for the children.

The school's scores have remained consistently high in succeeding years and so it was that *"By the summer of 2007 the school found itself in a position where it felt able to develop a curriculum that reflected more closely the ethos and philosophy of the school."*

Back to the Question

As schools stand on the cusp of deciding whether to launch into a radical reform of their curriculum, it is often the dilemma of SATs which provokes the question *"Does the creative curriculum raise standards?"* If it does then all is well as there is a marrying of the government's desire to "raise standards" and the school's desire to deliver a creative curriculum. If it does not raise scores, or worse sets them into decline, then schools will be reticent to put themselves in a position where they become vulnerable to the expectations of those who judge their performance, be this through the league tables or Ofsted inspections.

Having returned recently from an educational study visit in Slovakia it has become clear that the issue is not one that is uniquely UK based. In 2008 the Slovak government published a curriculum that they trusted would bring creativity to schools. On paper it was exemplary, was welcomed by schools and set in train a series of initiatives that engendered a high level of creativity within schools. Unfortunately the inspection process continued to inspect schools on a skewed version of the New Curriculum using the non-statutory guidance to judge schools on the more traditional elements. Almost overnight curriculum development spluttered, stalled and then virtually halted as the realities of the accountability machine suppressed the desire to innovate.[26] The truth is we live in an educational landscape where we need to deliver those things that external stakeholders demand and ultimately judge us against.

[26] *School reform, changes in curriculum in Slovakia - M. Kríž, Deputy head of the National Institute for Education*

Raising Standards in SATs

As you can imagine my own answer to the question of "raising standards" is greatly coloured by my own experience. Firstly, I do not think there is a direct correlation between a creative curriculum and a corresponding increase in the standards of the core subjects. If this were the case then the Wyche would not have needed to pursue a different journey to get to its current position. In the year 2000 the school was creative (although maybe not as much as it is now) but this was not enough to deliver good SAT results. Those of us who have worked with SATs over the years are well aware that good, creative scientists who were proficient in AT1 have no possibility of expressing this in a written test. The same is true of our most creative mathematicians who can explore, theorise and develop hypotheses in lessons, but find there is no opportunity for this creative flair to be brought out in a 45 minute test on number crunching. The reality is that the SAT tests are not there to test creativity they are there to test the basic fundamental skills within given subjects. The Wyche needed one solution to solve the SAT issue and another to develop greater creativity within the curriculum.

Raising Standards in Teaching and Learning

Leaving behind the debate regarding SATs, the broader question remains *Does the creative curriculum raise standards in the National Curriculum subjects?* Again my answer would be "maybe" and not a definite affirmation that it will.

As with all schools we have sought to raise standards in Numeracy and Literacy. To facilitate this we have moved away from the National Strategies and developed our own frameworks in both subjects. The school has written two documents that seek to improve the teaching and learning of Mathematics; these have driven standards higher throughout the school and their constant refinement allows for further progress.[27] In Literacy the

---

[27] *In 2010 the Year 6 children undertook the KS3 Maths paper as well as the statutory KS2 SAT test. 50% of the children attained level 6 and 25% scored level 7*

school has its own "Pedagogy for Writing" document which is delivering high standards in both key stages.[28] Whilst these documents[29] were written to raise standards in these core areas, it is important to remember that the Wyche curriculum was not designed specifically for that purpose.

The Wyche curriculum was developed as "The School Curriculum" and in the words of the National Curriculum was intended, as we have seen, to provide a cohesive framework for *all learning and other experiences that each school plans for its pupils.*" Its remit was broad and designed to subsume the teaching of the national curriculum subjects in a structure that delivered something larger than simply a set of subject based skills. Even a superficial reading of the Wyche Curriculum would lead one to conclude that its primary focus rests on the personal development of the child as both a learner and as a person rather than any specific curriculum subject area. Indeed the National Curriculum has two core aims which underpin all that is to be taught. Whilst the first relates to a more traditional view of learning: *The school Curriculum should aim to provide opportunities for all pupils to learn and achieve.* The second bears no resemblance to anything particularly academic and states that schools should: *promote pupil's spiritual, moral, social and cultural development and prepare all pupils for the opportunities, responsibilities and experiences of life.* On this basis one could argue that the National Curriculum itself is designed to do much more than simply raise standards in a range of given subjects.

What I am saying is this, if I was on a desert island with a class of children and was allowed, in the great tradition of that well known radio programme, to take one book with me, besides the bible and the complete works of Shakespeare – which book would I take? The simple answer is that if I wished to raise standards in Mathematics then I would take our Numeracy documents. If I was seeking to improve Literacy skills I would take the Writing Documents but if I wished to develop a sense of community and well being amongst the children I would take the Wyche Curriculum. I am quite sure it is possible to fry an egg on a hand dryer but

---

[28] *In 2011 81% of the children attained Level 5 at KS2*
[29] *All these documents can be found on the school website: http://www.wyche.worcs.sch.uk/*

it is not what it was designed for. Use a frying pan to fry an egg and a hand dryer to dry your hands and life would appear to be a lot more straightforward. It may be possible to raise standards of Numeracy and Literacy through the school curriculum but that is not what it was primarily designed for.

Recently I found myself in a forum discussing curriculum innovation with a number of colleagues predominantly from the secondary sector. Their rationale, virtually without exception, was that they wanted to establish a curriculum that was centred on competencies with the sole purpose of raising standards in each curriculum subject and consequently increasing scores in GCSE scores. Whilst I find the aspiration laudable (back to Ken Robinson's comment: *Who would want to lower standards?*), I fear that they might be using the wrong tool to achieve their goal. Surely a competency based curriculum is primarily designed to develop greater abilities in a range of competencies, not to deliver higher SAT results or GCSE scores.

Many point to the fact that there appears to be a direct correlation between those schools deemed to be successful and those that have developed an innovative curriculum. Whilst this may well be true it does not mean that the inverse is true namely that if all schools were to develop a creative curriculum then all schools would be successful. The realities of educational success are far more complex than this seemingly simplistic link. There is a danger that we buy into the notion that developing a creative curriculum will raise standards in subjects but I would question this premise.

As I stated at the outset maybe we are asking the wrong question, maybe the question should be: *Is the Creative Curriculum the best method of raising standards in Numeracy and Literacy?* For me the answer is unequivocal and I would suggest there are better options to take if this is your end goal. If this is the case then I am sure some might well respond by saying: *Is the any point developing a creative curriculum?* However, this might be like asking whether there is any use developing a hand dryer if it cannot fry an egg.

The rationale behind the development of the Wyche Curriculum was not founded on a need, or indeed a desire, to raise standards in any particular subject area. It sprung from a belief that children need a wider, broader and all inclusive skill set if they are to flourish in the technological age in which they live. To this end the school is not primarily interested if standards are raised in other subjects. The key question with regards to the Wyche Curriculum should be: *Is it raising standards in each child's ability to relate to others, helping them understand themselves and manage their learning in a wide range of increasingly complex situations.*

Is there any link between a Creative Curriculum and Standards?

The stance taken so far would seem to imply that there is no correlation between a creative curriculum and standards attained across the curriculum as a whole, yet research would appear to demonstrate otherwise. I concede that there may well be a relationship between the quality of curriculum provision and attainment; however, it would be my contention that if it does exist it is generic to the learning process and not related to specific subjects.

We must not confuse the creative curriculum with that of creative teaching. The latter has existed in the hands of competent professionals since time immemorial. It is therefore beyond question that the teacher who is able to engage children through natural enthusiasm or lessons that remain memorable will be more effective than the rather dour copying from the board many of us might remember from our own school days. However, the creative curriculum is not about creative lessons, not even about creative teaching, it is about encasing the learning in a curriculum that delivers on a macro scale. We have always had creative teachers, who have delivered creative lessons, what has been missing has been the all encompassing curriculum values which enrich learning holistically.

The "Big Picture"[30] (QCA) sought to look at the curriculum in this context. The Wyche Curriculum too addresses the issues of curriculum development in it broadest sense. Its focus is on the child rather than attainment and looks to address their needs as a learner and as a person rather than a historian, geographer or mathematician. For too long our focus in education has been on the micro elements such as the outstanding lesson or the good teacher. The concept of Curriculum Innovation allows us to reflect on the larger scale issues such as what children truly need to thrive in the society of the 21st century.

What might be true and may also be objectively quantifiable is the progress that each child makes both in terms of their understanding of themselves and others and their ability to manage their own learning. It is generally accepted that the best teachers are those who foster the richest relationships with children and create a classroom climate that engenders productive learning.[31] Where children's relationships thrive they work well together and feed off one another academically as well as emotionally and socially. Where self esteem is high and constructive group work is strong, opportunities for learning thrive as children learn not just from the teacher but in discussion and evaluation of their work with their peers.

There can be little doubt, simply because common sense tell us it is so, that a classroom where relationships between teacher and pupils are strong and children feel at ease working with each other, will have a greater impact on learning than one where this is not present. It is these attributes that the "School Curriculum" (as opposed to the National Curriculum) seeks to deliver. They are the means by which the aims, values and ethos of the school are engendered and rooted within the whole school. This will undoubtedly have a direct knock on effect on standards in every subject. But what is vital to appreciate is that this is a by-product of a competency based curriculum, not its raison d'être.

---

[30] *http://www.qcda.gov.uk/resources/publication.aspx?id=aaf9d7bf-7043-4bd8-9bb8-438d36908984*
[31] *Hay McBer (2000) Models of Teacher Effectiveness, DfEE*

CHAPTER 6

ASSESSING THE SOCIAL CURRICULUM: THE JOURNEY SO FAR

The School Curriculum

In 2007 The Wyche developed a curriculum that sought to draw out the ethos of the school and set it into a format that would underpin all the teaching within the school, and create a fresh focus for the day to day learning of the children. The curriculum is founded on 4 key areas: Relating to Self, Relating to Others, Managing Learning and Managing Situations. The emphasis is firmly centered on personal and social attributes and the development of skills set in the context of real life learning.

The Thorny Issue of Assessment

Whilst the establishment of anything new has a natural complexity in terms of change management it would be fair to say that the development of the curriculum was fairly straight forward when set against the requirement to assess the children's progress within it. The school found itself sailing into the unchartered waters of personal and social assessment and seeking to define this in terms of progress for individual children. There is little research available in this area and therefore any work would be definition be innovative in its nature, something Jim Rose recognised in his recommendations for the proposed Primary Curriculum[32] when he stated that *"Personal development together with literacy, numeracy and*

---

[32] *Independent Review of the Primary Curriculum: Final Report April 2009*

*ICT constitute the essentials for learning and life. The DCSF should work with the QCA to find **appropriate and innovative ways of assessing pupils' progress** in this area. (emphasis mine)*

The Issues

In its desire to be open to fresh and new approaches the school ended up travelling into many cul-de-sacs before charting its current path. The following areas were considered and discounted:

i. **Criterion Referenced:** Probably because the rest of the curriculum is founded on this approach the school initially sought to develop criteria that would outline progression in a series of levels. It soon became obvious that whilst academic progress may have natural stages that are generally linear in terms of progression there is a far greater complexity in assessing aspects such as a child's self esteem.

ii. **Norm Referenced:** A similar scenario occurred when we looked at seeking to establish norms for a given group of children and assessing children against their peers. The reality is that if one is measuring areas such as confidence then the issue becomes more one of context than of an attribute in isolation. There will be plenty of areas in life where we all feel confident and yet if we were to find ourselves in a different environment we might discover our supposed confidence heavily challenged.

iii. **The Assessment:** Related to the two points above it became clear that any assessment could not be summative in the sense that it could be "tested". Any assessment can only be performance and outcome based and must be inferred from actions, behaviours and choices. Those who teach the Foundation Stage will readily recognise this practice as an integral aspect of assessment within any good Reception class, however, to teachers further up the school this may well be a different way of looking at the assessment issue.

iv. **Assessing in a Social Context:** By definition social and emotional assessment needs to occur in a social and emotional setting. This means that the child will be in a group rather than an individual context. So if we are seeking to assess a child's leadership skills we need to factor in a group element. A child might indeed be showing great leadership strengths in a given group but this may be more an assessment of the biddable nature of the peers they have chosen to work with rather than his/her exceptional ability to galvanise others.

v. **The Influence of Relational Context:** As well as the context of the task, there is also the relational context. We all tend to feel more confident and more resilient towards a task if we undertake it alongside those with whom we feel safe to share and express ideas and where relationships are strong. Similarly I may feel more secure about a task where I personally have confidence in the ability of the other team members to fulfil their elements of the project.

vi. **Linear Assessment:** By its nature social and emotional assessment is not linear. Whilst one may recognise in academic performance that the child who has mastered tens and units in Mathematics will next be introduced to hundreds, this is not the case in emotional development. As stated previously confidence may ebb and flow due to a variety of factors but this does not mean that the child is not making good progress emotionally. For instance, the opinionated, arrogant child may flounder in a group of similar strong minded peers and may appear on the surface to have "lost his/her confidence" but we all know that it is the challenge of the context that is driving the emotional learning forward.

vii. **Holistic Approach:** It soon becomes evident that assessment in traditional terms was going to be a non-starter. Also any system that moved towards a "tick box" type of assessment to demonstrate a form of progression was at best going to be superficial and at worse philosophically flawed. The reality is that assessment should be driven by the curriculum, yet as we know to our cost, all too often it is the assessment that drives the curriculum. It is crucial, especially in this area of social assessment, that schools do not develop assessment structures that turn in on themselves so that teachers chase the assessment rather than the emotional development of the child. The truth is that tick boxes often lead to "Curriculum Dissonance" rather than creating a sense of "Curriculum Coherence". There is always the danger that teachers strive to chase the assessment and not the purity of the learning.

The Answer found in the Problem

In short there is a complexity about this area which should not be underestimated. In seeking to assess a child's emotional performance in a given activity the teacher needs to be aware that their ability to perform effectively will be affected by the task itself, those undertaking it with him, as well as other emotional influences from the basics of tiredness and hunger through to the personal issues brought into school from the outside; all of which have the ability to impinge on their performance.

It soon became apparent that there was probably no way any teacher could make an effective assessment of the child's emotional well-being at any point in time. But out of this apparent dead end came the opening up of a fresh solution. If teachers, who in a school context are those who know the child as well as anyone, cannot assess a child's well being then maybe there is only one person who can give an accurate description of their progress and that is the child themselves.

The Principle of the Learning Logs

With our understanding now centred on a view that the assessment process should develop from the child, our thinking started to move towards a model where the development and assessment could fuse together in the mind of the child. We started to explore the concept that it was the child that should assess their own needs based on previous performance and then seek to make a statement themselves about their own future development. A point Jim Rose drew out in "The Independent Review of the Primary Curriculum" where he states that *"Assessment is an integral aspect of all teaching and learning"* [33]

This was facilitated through the use of what the school has come to term "Learning Logs". These are, in essence, diaries where the children record their social progress, make assessments of their own performance in a

---

[33] *Independent Review of the Primary Curriculum: Final Report April 2009*

given group setting and then outline their own areas for improvement. Introduced into the Year 6 class they were used in the first instance at the beginning and ending of each term as a reflection journal and then a target setting process for the following term. This has progressed into a form where they are used on a more regular basis and have been fully integrated into the classroom ethos. They provide a reflective form of assessment and whilst they are not criterion or norm referenced in any way, they demonstrate a clear path of progression for each individual child.

The rationale behind the learning logs hinge on the belief that due to the deeply personal nature of social assessment only the child is fully able to chart their own way forward in terms of their next stage of learning. From this initial standpoint it appeared to us that the natural extrapolation of this philosophy was that the child in turn would be the person most empowered to understand what was required for them in their next phase of emotional development.

It was a year 6 child who blew the theory apart. Rebecca (not her real name) had found the last group project challenging; she had received feedback from her group that she was too bossy. To be fair to her she took the criticism on the chin and resolved in her Learning Log that she would…*"listen more to other people and their views as long as their views weren't totally stupid."* Is that not just everyone's version of bossy?! From this, and other similar instances, it became readily apparent that children need input to move their own emotional learning forward. We are well acquainted with this in an academic arena. Whilst self assessment may be a key area in the process of learning, the emphasis on formative assessment and effective teacher feedback in recent years has shown that the strategic input of the teacher moves the learning forward apace.[34] As Bruner points out learning is facilitated by those who scaffold the process for the child and offer both correction and the charting of a fresh way forward. Whilst my initial thoughts were that emotional learning was too complex and deeply personal for external processing it is evident that Bruner's theory applies as much to emotional as it does to academic learning.

---

[34] *Hattie, J (2009) Visible Learning*

The success of the Learning Logs therefore hinge on two strategic pieces of feedback in conjunction with that of the child themselves:

i. **Peer Assessment:** The learning logs are not just completed by the child but by the peers in the group they have worked with. Their insight is essential; the truth is that we enter a "fight or flight" mode when we feel emotionally criticised. It is all too apparent that whilst human nature can cope reasonably tolerably with criticism about "the things they do" (rationalising this as external to them as a person), we find criticism about "who we are" desperately personal and tend to view this as a personal attack; therefore, we build protective behaviours around us. The propensity for self deception is very strong. For effective emotional development to occur there needs to be clear and accurate feedback given to each child by those they have worked alongside them. It goes without saying that the key to any success in this area lies in the climate of support that the teacher has built within the classroom culture, as without it relationships will splinter and implode. However, when this is securely in place we have seen children make positive and tangible emotional progress which in turn has had a major impact upon their learning in all areas of the curriculum.

ii. **Teacher Assessment:** Whilst peer assessment is a vital element in the process it may still engender a scenario where the child knows what is wrong but cannot fathom out how to correct or modify their behaviour. The teacher holds a key role in this regard. Firstly they are required on occasions to mediate the views of the peers to the child, exploring and effectively interpreting the feedback for them. Secondly they are in the ideal position as the pastoral and emotional mentor of the child to talk through some of the issues with them and provide alternative ways forward for any succeeding project work they might undertake.

Summary Statement

Alongside a classroom culture where the child feels "emotionally safe" with both the classteacher and consequently with their peers, these two forms of input can provide a major springboard for emotional development. The key factor as with all learning is that the child should gain ownership of the whole process, seeing the role of the teacher and peers as that of a "critical friend" and key partners in their emotional journey. The school based evidence in the upper stages of Key Stage 2 (we have yet to take it lower in the school) is that the Learning Logs have become a powerful tool to drive forward the emotional development of children.

POSTSCRIPT
Assessing the Social Curriculum: The New Zealand Key Competencies

There would appear to be little research evidence world wide for the principles of social and emotional assessment, however, in the midst of its own locally based research on this subject the school came across the curriculum in New Zealand and more especially the research of two educationalists in particular; Margaret Carr and Rosemary Hipkins.

A revision of the National Curriculum was undertaken in 2007 in New Zealand. It is built around the understanding that children need more than just a narrow traditional academic diet to thrive in the "real world" of the 21st century. They developed a set of (what they call) "Key Competencies" which seek to reflect a more emotional, social and relational element to learning and put these at the heart of every learning experience of the child. Their curriculum states that:

"People use these competencies to live, learn, work, and contribute as active members of their communities. More complex than skills, the competencies draw also on knowledge, attitudes, and values in ways that lead to action... Opportunities to develop the competencies occur in social contexts. The competencies continue to develop over time, shaped by interactions with people, places, ideas, and things. Students need to be challenged and supported to develop them in contexts that are increasingly wide ranging and complex."
(Quote from The NZ curriculum p12)

There is recognition that the competencies and values are all encompassing and should therefore be embedded throughout the curriculum

"The key competencies are both end and means. They are a focus for learning – and they enable learning. They are the capabilities that young people need for growing, working, and participating in their communities and society. The school curriculum should challenge students to use and

develop the competencies across the range of learning areas and in increasingly complex and unfamiliar situations."

However, just as we have found at The Wyche the key issue remained the assessment of the competencies and finding ways to make judgements about each child's progress, the setting of further goals and the providing of evidence to demonstrate the effectiveness of the assessment process. In New Zealand the work on this has rested heavily on the thinking of Margaret Carr and Rosemary Hipkins.

Margaret Carr developed the concept of *"Learning Stories"*. Interestingly she worked primarily in early year settings and realised quickly that emotional development is too complex to be treated as a linear tick box assessment activity. Building on the thinking of "sociocultural" educational philosophy that describes learning *"as appropriated in authentic cultural locations, defining them as communities of practice"*,[35] Carr considered that the *"Learning Story"*, which offered a narrative approach to assessment, was the most cogent approach as it considered *"the context, location and people involved, as they all play a part in learning"*.

Rosemary Hipkins observed that whilst the concept of the "Transference of Learning" was a powerful assessment tool in academic learning to determine whether children could apply their learning in a variety of contexts, this principle was not transferable into an emotional and relational arena. Just because one has learnt a social skill set with one group of peers does not mean that the same would work with a fresh set of individuals. She also acknowledged that the assessment process *"needs to empower the learner to further develop their personal competencies"*[36]; concluding that *"more than one person should be involved in the judgement process"*. Using what she describes as a *"a new metaphor for assessment"* she drew on the work of Ginette Delandshere[37], who coined the phrase *"Assessment task as performance"*, and who's contention was the same as that of Margaret Carr that social assessment requires a 360

---

[35] *Carr, M. (2001) Assessment in Early Childhood Settings: Learning Stories.*
[36] *Hipkins R, (2007) Assessing the Key Competencies*
[37] *Ginette Delandshere (2002) Assessment as Enquiry*

degree approach that fleshes out everything in the 3-D of the real world and should not seek to reduce the complexity of the assessment to a two dimensional tick box. She advocated four possible approaches:

i.   Learning Journals: A very similar approach to that which we have adopted at The Wyche.
ii. Learning Stories: In line with Margaret Carr's thinking.
iii. Portfolios: These are collated annotated evidence of learning, similar to those that some schools have developed in the UK for evidence of progression in academic subjects.
iv. Rich Tasks: These were first developed as part of the New Basics curriculum in Queensland, Australia and involve engaging the children in a series of complex multi-faceted tasks which they work towards over time receiving formative feedback as they progress.

In considering all their research the New Zealand government thought it would be inappropriate to place pressure on schools to develop criterion or norm referenced assessments, or even to report on them formally:

"For good reasons, there is no requirement to assess and report the competencies. The requirement is to support students to develop them. The school's obligation is to explain and demonstrate how it is doing that and with what effect." (NZ National Curriculum p44)

What schools are encouraged to do is to *"...monitor the development of the key competencies. With appropriate teacher guidance and feedback, all students should develop strategies for self-monitoring and collaborative evaluation of their performance in relation to suitable criteria."*

To this end the Learning Logs of The Wyche would appear to dovetail well into this pedagogical framework providing a rich learning journal for each child's emotional development over a period of time.

CHAPTER 7

MANAGING THE PROCESS OF CHANGE

Managing the Process of Change

The leadership and management of curriculum change is complex because it will be determined by the unique set of circumstances that impinge on each school. Generic solutions to curriculum innovation are therefore futile for whilst they have the appearance of perceived wisdom they cannot deliver a bespoke solution to each and every school. I offer the following observations not as a model to follow but as broad brush stroke thoughts as a starting point for debate. They are a distillation of my thinking from the discussions I have had with others on this subject in recent years.

A National Step Forward: A Sea Change in Thinking

There has been a move nationally away from the heavy centralised model that dominated the educational landscape over the past few decades. The White Paper of 2005 boldly states that "schools are most effective when they have the autonomy to innovate and adapt to their local circumstances".[38] Indeed even prior to this the Excellence and Enjoyment document had already made it clear that *"teachers already have great freedoms to exercise their professional judgment about how they teach... and the government supports that"*[39] Balanced against this, and in seeming

---

[38] *Higher Standards, Better Schools For All (2006) DfEE*
[39] *Excellence and Enjoyment (2003) DfEE*

contradiction to it, there remains in place a model of national accountability that operates through the league tables and the Ofsted inspection regime. There can be little debate that schools must be seen to deliver on the agendas of stakeholders but there does appear to be opportunity for schools to explore fresh expressions of the curriculum. To be fair the Ofsted framework (2009) positively encourages schools to move along this road stating that the curriculum in outstanding schools should provide... *"memorable experiences and rich opportunities for high-quality learning and wider personal development and well-being. The school may be at the forefront of successful, innovative curriculum design in some areas."*[40] According to David Blunkett this may be a short lived window of opportunity. He remains sceptical that the current trend towards devolving authority to local schools will persist in the long term. As he confided to the Select committee *"I know we will move back again once people have discovered that you do need levers to pull if you want to change what is happening in classrooms"*[41]

A Potential Barrier: Leadership or Management?

Without wishing to appear derogatory to the many of us who have chosen the vocation of headship as a career we have tended as a profession to fall into the trap of managing the curriculum rather than leading it. Since the introduction of the National Curriculum we have got used to there being a central dictate with regards to the substance of the curriculum. In some measure it might be said that we have abdicated our responsibility to lead schools (although others might argue that this position has been usurped by successive governments) and that it is now the sole responsibility of the department of Education to determine the curriculum and its content. To a certain extent this is true, of course and the rationale behind the National Curriculum was to bring cohesion to what was taught throughout the country. However, there is a danger that headteachers see their role as "managers" rather then "leaders" of the curriculum. To clarify, many heads see their job as taking the national curriculum and "managing" how it is

---

[40] The evaluation schedule for schools (2009) Ofsted

[41] http://www.publications.parliament.uk/pa/cm200910/cmselect/cmchilsch/422/422.pdf

taught. They may monitor provision for groups of children, create lesson frameworks which provide high levels of differentiation and find creative ways of melding the subjects around topic headings, but essentially they are managing the curriculum they think is being imposed upon them rather than taking real ownership of it at a local level. What schools are crying out for are not managers but leaders; those who can see a vision not just for the social, economic and technological future but seek to shape a curriculum that reflects these trends thereby blending seamlessly with the needs of the learners.

It was John Abbot who first coined the phrase *"the teacher proof curriculum"*. He was commenting on the politician's response to, what they saw as, declining standards in the latter part of the last century. Their solution was to prescribe even in great detail not only the content of the curriculum but latterly through the national strategies how it was taught in schools. This in spite of Kenneth Clarke's quote when he was Education secretary that: *"Questions about how to teach are not for governments to decide"*. As John Abbot concluded this turned teaching from a profession to a trade overnight.[42] The result of such over-prescription was to drive the system towards mediocrity. I accept it may have assisted in turning unsatisfactory teachers into satisfactory practitioners, but conversely it tended to diminish the effectiveness of our best teachers as the system strove to deliver uniformity. The structure removed the autonomy of the teacher thereby depriving many of their greatest attribute, which is the ability to mould the teaching curriculum around the child rather than around, what the Cambridge Review described as *"the bland and pre-packaged government approved lessons"*.[43]

The standardisation agenda has so dominated our thinking that many of those in senior management have an overt fear of moving away from the guidelines and practices that many perceive as mandatory. When Mick Waters was head of QCA he toured the country giving, what he called, the "permissions message". He sought to demonstrate that even under the present national curriculum it is possible to inject great elements of

---

[42] *The Unfinished Revolution (2004) John Abbot and Terry Ryan*
[43] *Children their world their education (2009) Robin Alexander et.al.*

innovation successfully into the curriculum and yet remain within the legal framework of statutory provision. At one such seminar I found myself in a plenary discussion where the main topic of debate appeared to be whether QCA intended to publish "the creative curriculum" in a form we could all follow. The concept is a total contradiction in terms; the whole purpose of the message was not to engender a fresh level of governmental prescription, but to deliver the clear message to heads and school leaders that we are tasked with leading the curriculum in our own schools. Of course there are inbuilt challenges in that, but school leaders need to have a clear sense of moral purpose and a clear understanding of what they are seeking to build in their own particular schools. There is a danger that we consider it easier to abdicate our leadership responsibility and revert to the role of manager because it has become our default position for too long. It is teachers and headteachers who are the professionals and it is they who have the knowledge and understanding as to what children need to learn. George Tomlinson (minister for education in the 1940's) famously said *"The minister knows nowt about education"* and in one sense he is quite right, politicians are policy makers not experts in pedagogy. The truth is that the national curriculum itself, the White Paper and even the Ofsted framework are all seeking to move schools into an arena where they can design "a school curriculum". We should seize the opportunity with relish, taking the baton back from the politicians and delivering it back into the hands of our profession.

A Potential Barrier: Reformation or Revolution

As Ken Robinson has stated *"Every education system in the world is being reformed at the moment and it is not enough; reform is no use anymore because that is simply improving a broken model what we need is not evolution but revolution; this has to be transformed into something else".*[44] It is indeed not enough. The time has come to stand back from the curriculum developed for a Victorian age and determine for ourselves whether it remains fit for purpose in the 21st century.

---

[44] *http://www.ted.com/talks/sir_ken_robinson_bring_on_the_revolution.html*

If we are to truly innovate within the curriculum it is not enough to tinker around the edges of the current structure and inject a bit of creativity into it. The schools which are really at the cutting edge of curriculum innovation are those that are standing back, looking at the big picture and ascertaining how the national curriculum subjects can be dovetailed cohesively into a curriculum that delivers so much more. There is no value in anything less, indeed schools that have pursued the lesser path often become discouraged as they see initiatives failing to deliver. As has been said *"Frustration abounds amongst educators as some try to amend, adjust and revise within the tight confines of 19th Century structures. These efforts can actually make the problems worse as dissatisfaction arises."* [45]

It is argued by some that not all schools are ready for revolution and therefore need to be coaxed more gently along the creative continuum. However the question remains; is it possible to move gently towards total and complete transformational reform? The question is virtually rhetorical. What schools need is leaders who have the courage of their convictions, a clear pedagogical understanding of what they wish to achieve and can set this within a curricular framework that reflects a full appreciation of the social trends of the day. It is a high calling but anything less is not a creative curriculum, it is the same subject based curriculum with a bit more creativity sprinkled into it and that is not what is required in times of monumental global change.

A Potential Barrier: Personal vision and inner belief

Related to the debate on curriculum revolution is the need for any innovation in this regard to be underpinned by a deep sense of moral purpose. The centralisation of educational thinking has led many to see the curriculum as a disembodied concept and a collection of subjects and programmes of study. The real truth is that the curriculum should be a reflection of those who deliver it. This is easy to demonstrate on a micro scale; it is evident to all, that creative teachers deliver the curriculum in a creative way, dull teachers teach in a dull way. So too with the school

---

[45] *Curriculum 21 (2010), Heidi Hayes Jacob*

curriculum, its very essence will be a reflection of the aims, values and beliefs of the school leadership as they drive these deep into the fabric of their school. Ofsted have found that *"all outstanding headteachers had one factor in common, they all had a deep sense of moral purpose"*[46] It is this sense of moral purpose that that is the driving force behind a truly coherent school curriculum

Where schools try to adopt a curriculum without the engagement of the heart it will sadly fall at the first hurdle. The successful development of any initiative rests solely on the energy of those driving it forward and their energy derives from an all consuming, unshakable, inner belief in what they are seeking to achieve . It is this passionate commitment that pushes through the inevitable difficulties and problems that will undoubtedly arise.

I am often asked what I think of commercially produced curricula. For those who have followed my argument so far you will no doubt be able to second guess my response. My answer is two fold. Firstly there is the danger that it becomes another form of leadership abdication placing school leaders back into the role of curriculum manager rather than curriculum leader. However, more importantly, those who seek such solutions reveal a lack of understanding as to the key role of impassioned leadership in the driving forward of the school curriculum.

It was John Maxwell in his seminal work on leadership who made the point that *"People don't at first follow worthy causes. They follow worthy leaders who promote causes they can believe in. People buy into leaders first and then the leader's vision"*.[47] John West Burnham undertook a study of school leaders for the NCSL and his conclusions drew clear parallels with those of Maxwell *"Outstanding headteachers attribute their success to confidence growing out of personal values, professional relationships and rich learning experiences... It is impossible to separate the role of the leader from the leader as a person"*.[48] Schools are a direct reflection, for

---

[46] *The quote came from an address given by Christine Gilbert, head of Ofsted but the same sentiments are found in their document Twenty outstanding primary schools - Excelling against the odds (2010)*
[47] *Maxwell, J (1998) 21 irrefutable laws of leadership*

better or worse, of those who lead them; this is an immutable principle. So the curriculum of any school will be by definition a reflection of the ethos, aims and values of its leader – this is leadership.

It is this element that makes the School Curriculum so powerful. It is not just a tool for delivering a miscellany of arbitrary subjects to an unsuspecting cohort of children. It is something that derives from the heart of the leadership and is then evidenced throughout the school informally in its ethos and more formally in its curriculum. The curriculum should simply be viewed as the learning arm of the school with its underlying values. There should not be a disconnect between these two things the same as there was never intended to be a separation of the academic subjects from the two aims underpinning them within the framework of the National Curriculum.

Many, including members of my own staff have used the word "brave" to describe many of the actions we have taken to deliver the curriculum that is now firmly embedded in the school. The truth is whilst our apparent wish to swim against the tide of popular thinking might look like bravery it is not rooted in a desire just to appear to be counter culture, it is an expression of the values and ethos that runs deep through the life of the school. So in 2008-09 when some were struggling to plan and implement a pure form of the School Curriculum we took the option of establishing a moratorium on teaching any of the Foundation Subjects. This was perceived by many as a bold stance, and in truth it would have been interesting if Ofsted had come for an inspection of the subject we were not teaching that year! Whilst some attributed this to bravery (although I am sure others may have termed it as stupidity!) it was driven from a belief that we were building something greater and more important than whether we taught History in any given year.[49]

---

[48] West-Burnham, John, (2009), Developing Outstanding Leaders, NCSL
[49] I was of course aware that the Programmes of Study are required to be taught over a Key stage and there is nothing that prevents schools teaching all the History in one year should they wish. Interestingly enough the Danish primary curriculum has only three subjects that are taught every year, the others are taught in one given year within the Key stage. There is nothing in present legislation to prevent schools taking this as an option under the current National Curriculum.

We do have a propensity in education for what I term "layered change", meaning we tend to place each new initiative on the foundation of the last one. This means that over time we end up with copious layers of change which tend to overwhelm and frustrate the ability of any school to move forward. We need to develop a mindset which recognises the good that has got us to where we are but is not fearful of dispensing with any aspect that has become outdated or outmoded. It was evident that teachers well versed in the traditional view of curriculum planning needed their thinking dismantled totally before they would be able to take on a completely new structure. It is not always possible to build the new on the old, or as was once said *"You do not put new wine into old wineskins".*[50]

Whilst it is true the majority of successful schools have headteachers that might, in the words of the Hay McBer study, be called mavericks[51] they are not necessarily anti-establishment in principle. These heads have a vision that they feel supersedes the somewhat bland and generic national agendas. The introduction of the report states that *"There is a brand of leadership, active in schools today, which makes the establishment nervous. It is also leadership that delivers the results the establishment wants"*; noting that these headteachers had within them *"a willingness, in some instances a delight, in challenging assumptions."* However, there was an underlying motivation behind all they did because *"they are driven by a deep personal conviction that what they are doing is morally right".* This is wonderfully illustrated by the words of Alan Roach one of the headteachers who, whilst admitting that not all his initiatives were popular, observed that *"It took some people's breath away, and upset some people, but it had to be done."* It is that last sentence that expresses the heart of every successful school leader – *it had to be done.* These words are a window into the heart of a leader driven with an inner conviction which is unshakable and it is this that will transform schools and deliver to them a curriculum that is rich in terms of its aims, values and purpose.

---

[50] *The Gospel of Mark 2:22*
[51] *Maverick – Breakthrough Leadership that transforms schools (2002) Hay McBer*

BIBLIOGRAPHY

Abbot J and Ryan T (2004) The Unfinished Revolution

Alexander R. et al. (2009) Children their world their education

Carr, M. (2001) Assessment in Early Childhood Settings: Learning Stories.

Claxton, G. (2010) What is the point of School?

Heidi J. (2010) Curriculum 21

Damasio, A. (2006) Descartes Error

Delandshere, G. (2002) Assessment as Enquiry

DfEE (2006) Higher Standards, Better Schools For All

Gardner, H. (1993). Multiple intelligences: The theory in practice.

Gilbert, C. (2008) Vision Teaching and learning in 2020

Gillard, D. (2011) Education in England: a brief history

Goleman, D. (1995) Emotional Intelligence

Hattie, J. (2009) Visible Learning

Hay McBer (2002) Maverick - Leadership that transforms schools

Hay McBer (2000) Models of Teacher Effectiveness, DfEE

Hipkins, R. (2007) Assessing the Key Competencies

Independent Review of the Primary Curriculum: Final Report 2009

IPPR study (2006) Freedoms Orphans

LeDoux, J. (1999) The Emotional Brain

Nummela, R. and Caine, G. (1994) Making Connections

Maxwell, J. (1998) 21 irrefutable laws of leadership

School reform, changes in curriculum in Slovakia - M. Kríž,

Ofsted (2002) The Curriculum in Successful Primary Schools

Ofsted (2009) The evaluation schedule for schools

The Struggle for the Soul of the 21st Century Bill Clinton, December 14, 2001

Tony Blair Connecting the Learning Society: DfES(1997)

Ofsted (2010) Twenty outstanding primary schools - Excelling against the odds

West-Burnham, J. (2009), Developing Outstanding Leaders, NCSL

White, J. (2004) Rethinking the School Curriculum

White, J. (2005) Towards an aims led curriculum

Geoff Rutherford

Geoff Rutherford has been the Headteacher at The Wyche School in Malvern since April 2000. Previous to that he taught in Kent, Somerset and Canada. The Wyche has been graded "Outstanding" twice by Ofsted and has gained an increasing reputation for its innovative curriculum. This has opened up opportunities to share and disseminate good practice. Whilst the school's website hosts much of his material, he also lectures to students in universities, addresses teacher's conferences as well as providing training in School Leadership for the NCSL. Whilst not claiming to be particularly well travelled he has visited Germany, Slovakia and Finland to look at the school systems in these countries. Despite all this his heart and passion remains in the classroom and to this end he continues to teach most days in classes throughout the school.

FURTHER INFORMATION ON THE WYCHE CURRICULUM CAN BE FOUND AT WWW.WYCHE.WORCS.SCH.UK

Printed in Great Britain
by Amazon

19894885R00047